Chinese New Year
Festivals

Chinese New Year Festivals

A Picturesque Monograph of the Rites, Ceremonies and
Observances in relation thereto

By JULIET BREDON

Author of "Peking" and "The Moon Year" (in collaboration)

Six Illustrations in Colour-photogravure from Selected Chinese Paintings

GRAHAM BRASH
SINGAPORE

© *Graham Brash, all revisions, 1989*

First Published in 1930

This revised edition first published in 1989 by
Graham Brash (Pte) Ltd
227 Rangoon Road
Singapore 0821

Reprinted, 1990

ISBN 9971-49-124-9

Printed in Singapore by
General Printing Services (Pte) Ltd

Chinese New Year Festivals

THE Chinese New Year, as celebrated according to the old "Moon Calendar," is a seasonal feast. Moreover from time immemorial different dynasties have varied the date for beginning the year to suit themselves. The *Hsia* Calendar (2205–1784 B.C.) adopted the first Spring moon as the equivalent of our January; the *Shang* Calendar (1783–1135 B.C.) the third Winter moon; the *Chou* Calendar (1134–247 B.C.) the second Winter moon, and the *Ch'in* Calendar (246–141 B.C.) the first Winter moon.

It is interesting to note that after all these alterations, the *Hsia* Calendar, worked out by the earliest Chinese astronomers so many centuries before Christ, was finally reverted to (in 140 B.C.) and is still widely used to-day not only among the Chinese themselves but to some extent by races like the Japanese and Koreans who adopted their culture.

When the primitive settlers of the "Middle Kingdom" changed from hunters and herdsmen to farmers, they considered the year as a cycle of crops. The seasons of sowing and reaping became, as it were, the pivots of the calendar. Therefore *THE* great festival was fixed at the time when Nature showed the first faint signs of awakening from her long winter sleep. This to a primitive agricultural people was the true New Year, season of re-birth, and they reckoned the date of its beginning to fall on the first day of the first new moon after the sun enters Aquarius; that is to say on a day not earlier than our January 21st and not later than our February 19th. The variation in the actual date of New Year's day is due to the fact that the lunar year sometimes has twelve and sometimes thirteen moons. Once every three years, twice every five years, or almost exactly seven times every nineteen years, an intercalary "moon" (which always has the same name as the month it follows) is added "for the purpose of making true time agree with the divisions of the calendar." How and why this is done involves tedious technical details. Suffice it to say, that, as a result of such intercalations, the Chinese "moon calendar" gives a surprisingly accurate division of the year, especially from the farmer's point of view. It also corresponds to weather conditions in a way that seems almost uncanny. When an extra winter "moon" appears in the calendar, there is invariably a longer spell of cold, whereas a double "moon" in summer means that the heat will be twice as intense as usual.

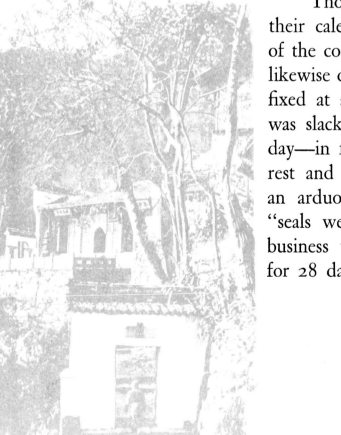

Those far seeing scholars, who fitted their calendar so well to the requirements of the country and the needs of the people, likewise decreed that the New Year Festival, fixed at a season when work in the fields was slack, should last longer than a single day—in fact should be a lengthy period of rest and pleasure before the beginning of an arduous year. Under the Empire the "seals were closed," that is to say official business was suspended as far as possible, for 28 days and most state dignitaries were

2

A Chinese home "dressed" for New Year

given leave to visit their homes. This privilege was all the more valued because officials were not allowed to serve in their own provinces and frequently their families did not accompany them to their distant posts.

Re-union under the ancestral roof was one of the fundamental New Year customs. "A cat in a strange garret, a bird with a broken wing, a fish out of water, are not more restless and unhappy than a Chinese who cannot go home at New Year time." Deep down at its roots, the old fashioned New Year was, and remains, a family festival. To be together in confidence and affection—no less deeply felt because undemonstratively expressed according to Western ideas—to feast in common; to worship the Gods and reverence the Ancestors; to wipe off old debts and start a clean slate, morally and materially, such were the underlying desires of every man and woman when the New Year was born.

Though these main features of the "great feast" existed throughout this vast country which is China, local customs as regards the celebrations of the holiday varied somewhat. In one province certain rites were performed on certain dates. They might take place a few days earlier or later in another. For example the first holiday ceremony of the *La Pa Chow*, a picturesque feast that has been adopted by the Buddhists as a religious festival, may be held on the 8th of the twelfth moon, on the 7th, or on the 10th. Even the legends of its origin vary. In the north people say that it began because of an old woman who had an unfilial son, a rarity and a disgrace in China. As this lad refused to provide food for his mother she,

4

partly to support herself and partly to make him "lose face" before the neighbours, went round with a begging bowl from house to house. At every door she received something, here a handful of rice, yonder some dried plums and further on millet, nuts, etc. These ingredients she cooked together into a Chinese version of our Christmas pudding, and modern housewives still copy her recipe, making enough for their own use as well as for gifts to relatives and friends.

In Central China the *La Pa Chow* becomes the *La Pa Nie* and is explained in a less poetic way. During the fortnight before New Year people, who feel the urge of generosity at the approach of the festive season, send presents of long white cakes called *Nie Kor* to one another. A popular family with many friends soon receives more of these cakes than can be used. How to get rid of them without being wasteful, an unforgivable sin in China, is the problem. It would not be tactful to invite the neighbours to eat stale dainties. Therefore on a certain day sanctioned by custom it is permissible to cut all these left over and dust covered cakes into small pieces, cook them with rice soup and cabbage, add a meat sauce to give the broth a flavour, and offer it as a gift. Sent before noon on *La Pa Nie*, or "Stock Pot Day," this mess of pottage is supposed to announce good luck.

For several weeks previous to the actual New Year holidays every Chinese kitchen is a scene of busy activity and poor indeed is the home where the stove is cold in the twelfth moon, for food is one of the important features of a Chinese holiday.

5

Indeed a feast celebrates every event in the people's lives—the building of a new house, the opening of a shop, the shaving of a baby's head. To "eat good things" is the colloquial expression for a wedding or a funeral, and there is a popular proverb which says, "During the first part of the first month no one has an empty mouth." The continuous New Year feasting is a keen joy to a nation forced from necessity, in the majority of cases, to live on frugal fare. Indeed the change from a diet which rarely includes meat, and the temporary let down of self control which seldom allows a man to eat his fill, are pleasures looked forward to throughout the twelve-month.

Among the peasants those families too poor to buy supplies join what are called "New Year Societies." Members pay small dues for the first five months of the year and meanwhile the money is put out at the high rates of interest—as much as five per cent a month —which prevail until the first harvest is in. After that the loans are repaid and the money invested in cakes and other holiday dainties that are distributed according to the needs of those who contributed to the society.

During the last seven days of the old year every house is given a thorough cleaning. Mother and daughter-in-law work side by side, their heads enveloped in cotton cloths. Both are careful to avert their eyes when the dust whirls out of neglected corners. They believe that a tiny human being lives in each eye and this minute creature may be killed by even a grain of dust.

New brooms must be used for the New

6

爆竹生花
王承熙
（印）

Firing crackers in honour of the Kitchen God

Year sweeping and handled with due reverence. The Chinese say that the broom is a member of the family. It is therefore never allowed to lie upon the ground, but must be kept leaning against a wall and picked up at once if it falls down.

When every room is spick and span, the best curios are put out and the handsomest scrolls and pictures the family possesses hung on newly papered walls. Someone is then sent to the flower shop to buy the plants which are an indispensable part of the New Year decorations. Dwarf fruit trees forced into blossom for the occasion, "Heavenly Bamboos" thick with red berries, fragrant orange and lemon trees, and the curious "Buddha's Fingers" shaped like folded hands, are favourites. Very seldom do we find cut flowers used.

Once the home is looking its best and ready to receive guests, it is important that it be protected against evil influences. This is done by means of "lucky inscriptions" which must be changed once a year. The old scarlet papers pasted on door frames and window sills are carefully taken down and new ones put in their places, for their power to keep away bad spirits is supposed to wear out. In a world where devils wait round every corner to catch the careless napping, it behoves wise householders to renew their hostages to good fortune. When the peddlers of luck posters come down the street calling out "Buy the scrolls of fortune, buy the pictures of the protecting gods," only the deaf turn inattentive ears.

Very old and very curious is the origin of the "*Chih ma,*" or rough portraits of the gods, and the "*tui tzu*" or red paper scrolls generally used in pairs for home protection. So long ago as the time of the Five Rulers

8

a New Year sacrifice was made to Heaven—a double sacrifice of thanksgiving and repentance. As a symbol of the latter the people smeared the posts and lintels of their doorways with the blood of a sacrificed lamb just as the Jews did at the season of the Passover.

Ages passed and paper was invented. Then, instead of blood, red paper was used on doors and gates. A curious survival in certain southern provinces is the mixture of sheep's blood and plaster, still popular for colouring wooden doorposts and window frames.

The first "*tui tzu*" were made of plain paper. It was only much later that characters were inscribed on them from purely decorative motives. The first couplets expressed thanks, those of modern days ask blessings, wealth, happiness, and good fortune.

The use of lucky inscriptions nowadays has grown to cover all a man's possessions instead of being confined to the doors and windows of a house. Small red luck papers appear upon the well and the cart, the plough and the pack saddle, the mast-head of a junk and the collar of a coal-carrying camel.

Of very special significance are the portraits of the "guardian gods" pasted on front gate panels. A few years ago these were universal, at least in the north, but they are going out of fashion since the police campaign, intended to root out popular superstitions, has forbidden them. Dying yet by no means dead, especially in the country districts, these pictured warriors were born of a legend that will live in the memories of the people long after their gaudy portraits have disappeared.

The original gate guardians were two good spirits who dwelt under a peach tree and vanquished demons by throwing them to tigers. But these hazy figures gave place to two generals of the great T'ang Emperor *T'ai T'sung* who lived in the seventh century A.D. Successful in so many undertakings, this mighty sovereign failed in his expedition to conquer Korea and his failure kept him awake at night. Evil dreams inspired by evil spirits tormented him and ugly devils crowded about his uneasy couch. Then two of his bravest warriors, men that feared neither mortal nor spiritual foe, volunteered to stand guard at the palace gates and keep the devils out. For many nights they watched successfully and His Majesty enjoyed a sound and dreamless sleep; but they could not go on indefinitely without rest as even an Autocratic Ruler realised. Now China has always been, in certain things, a "land of make believe." The "sign for the thing signified," often suffices. Paper effigies of servants and possessions satisfy the dead, paper money deceives the gods. Therefore His Majesty hit upon the happy idea of having the portraits of his warriors painted in full panoply of war. "Let them be pasted upon my gates," *T'ai T'sung* commanded, "and let care be taken that their weapons point away from each other in order that they may guard efficiently in both directions." Believe it or not the devils respected the pictures as they did the originals and kept away. So that is how the generals came to be gate gods and, from protectors of the palace, were adopted to guard the homes of the people.

Of all the heavenly portraits and earthly talismans that must be renewed at the New Year, the most important is that of the *Tsao Wang*, or Kitchen God, who presides over every home in China. On

10

The New Year altar ready for the "Essential Ceremonies"

the 23rd or the 24th of the twelfth moon this worthy ascends to Heaven and makes his report to the Jade Emperor, or Supreme Deity, on the behaviour of the household in which he lives. His going and coming are great events and must be suitably celebrated.

Tsao Wang himself is a picturesque figure portrayed now in one form, now in another. Usually he appears as an old man with his old wife beside him, a faithful soul who tried to save his life when he jumped into the oven but only managed to pull his legs out. Hence the legend that the fire tongs are *Tsao Wang's* legs. A horse often stands beside this venerable couple for use on journeys, but sometimes, if the charger is absent, the cockroaches which abound in many Chinese kitchens are supposed to serve as "*Tsao Wang's* horses."

The origin of the "Guardian of the Hearth" is wrapped in mystery. When and where he actually came into being is unkown. Some say he was once a mortal, others that he succeeded to the mantle of a much older divinity, perhaps a god of fire, but two things concerning him are certain; that he is one of the most antique of the Chinese gods, and one of the best beloved. Taoists and Buddhists have both adopted him into their Pantheons and he is still worshipped

in almost every Chinese family. The people look upon him as a kind of benevolent spy and before he departs to make his report on their behaviour, do their best to propitiate him. Some rub the lips of his portrait with honey or sugar in order that he may say sweet things only. Some wet them with wine to make him cheery and tolerant, and all alike prepare him as good a "departure feast" as they can possibly afford.

12

At the propitious hour when he is due to start, his portrait, taken down off the kitchen wall, is carried out into the courtyard either in its shrine or in a miniature sedan chair. A feast is offered him on an improvised altar and—in addition to food—candles, wine, and a ladder made of yellow paper are presented for the comfort of his journey. With incense torches to illuminate his road, *Tsao Wang* goes off in a chariot of fire, his picture being set alight by a flame from his own oven. Meanwhile, dried beans are thrown on the kitchen roof to imitate the sound of his horse's hoofs, and straw and tea are provided for his faithful steed.

Curiously enough it is the men not the women who say the prayers for the lucky voyage and safe return of the Hearth God. Although the kitchen is the wife's province, it is her husband who bids him farewell and greets him when he comes back. Why? No one seems able to explain. Perhaps because *Tsao Wang* is too important a personage to be seen off by any but the Master of the House.

The Kitchen God is supposed to remain away for seven days gossiping with the rulers of heaven and while he is absent the household breathes freely. Ordinary restraints are relaxed. The women may comb their hair in the kitchen if they feel like it—a thing strictly forbidden when he is at home. They may spit towards the oven, or do a dozen unsanitary things that are taboo the rest of the year. How many hygienic measures have been enforced by all religions in the name of their gods!

The service to *Tsao Wang* concludes, as most ceremonies do in China, with a salvo of fire crackers which, like so many other apparently inconsequential things, have an inner meaning. Their origin dates back into the dim past when a report of the doings of each family was written on pieces of bamboo, read to the gods by the head of the house, and afterwards burned. These "bamboo documents," when set alight, made a crackling sound. Hence the name "bamboo cracker" still commonly used for the modern fire cracker which only came into existence in its present form centuries later when a Taoist alchemist discovered how to make gun powder.

The Chinese themselves say that fire crackers and fireworks are useful for four purposes:

1. To terrify bad spirits by their noise and drive devils away.
2. To summon peace in the same way as the obsolete "Peaceful Drum."
3. To welcome the gods and good spirits at the New Year.
4. To attract prosperity and riches during the coming twelve-month.

Now money plays an important part in the New Year festival. Depending on suitable sacrifices to the Gods, and especially to the God of Wealth, a man believes he will be lucky or unlucky in his business ventures. Moreover, before the New Year dawns outstanding accounts must be closed and debts paid. The Chinese live largely on credit and only settle up what they owe three times a year; at the Dragon Festival, the 5th of the fifth moon; at the Harvest Festival, the 15th of the eighth moon; and at the end of the twelfth moon. Ready cash before the New Year is so

14

A New Year game of dice known as 鄉狀元 (*attaining the senior wranglership*)

essential to the credit of a business or an individual that there is a terrible scramble among all classes to get it. Men have been known to steal in order to satisfy their creditors, yet the theft was excused because it saved their financial reputations.

To be dunned in China is no disgrace. Few people even if able to pay, will do so until pressed. But at New Year the gentle persuasion sanctioned by custom gives place to drastic methods. Rich folks are threatened till they "lose face" before the neighbours; poor creditors co-erced by curses and even blows. A man has a right to camp on his debtor's doorstep till the latter hands over what he owes. In extreme cases he may be pursued even on New Year's morning with a lighted lantern. Though no money is supposed to change hands after dawn on the "first day," and one who evades his creditors till then is technically free till the Dragon festival, the light indicates to all concerned that it is still dark, therefore still the night before when debts may legally be collected. Harassed beyond bearing, a person without resources used to take refuge in the temple of the City God where theatrical performances went on continuously for several days. As custom permitted no one to interrupt the play, a ne'er-do-well could not be arrested so long as he remained in the sanctuary of the theatre-temple.

With luck, a firm or family decently concluded their settlement before "Watch Night," which corresponds to our New Year's Eve. People then had free time for bathing and dressing in new clothes, the women putting on their brightest silks and satins and arranging their hair elaborately with fresh flowers, the

16

children donning scarlet suits, "tiger caps" and "pussy shoes" with real whiskers sewn on them. Between these various occupations, some hours were snatched for sleep. For from sundown on the last day of the dying year till sunrise on the first day of the new, all were supposed to remain awake. To dose off even in one's own house was tactless, but to do so in the house of a relative or friend augured positive bad luck to host and guest.

It was, however, most unlikely that the latter should happen since only exceptional circumstances allowed a person to be under any roof but his own at the dawning of the New Year. In country districts where old customs are still rigidly enforced, even a widowed daughter who lives habitually in her parents' house may not stay there between 11 p.m. and 1 a.m. on the "Watch Night." This rule sometimes works great hardship when women and children are chased off the premises and obliged to walk the roads on a freezing winter night till sunrise when they are permitted to return. For in the old Chinese family cult a distinction is made between daughters who have once left the home and those who are still unmarried. Even a widow who may return to live with her own people, for economic or other reasons, still owes allegiance to the ancestor's of her late husband's house. Therefore she has no right to be present at the "essential ceremonies" which include sacrifices to the forefathers of her own family.

These "essential ceremonies" known as the "Triple Rites" in honour of Heaven and Earth, the Household Gods and the Spirits of the Dead, are performed twice—once before midnight as a farewell and once afterwards as a greeting.

Just before the first series take place the courtyards are carpeted with pine branches and the stalks of sesamun plants, the idea being that should devils come prowling about the house their footsteps on these dry plants would crackle and give warning of their presence. Next the well is closed and a promise made that no water will be drawn for twenty-four hours. This gives the God in charge a chance to go off duty and enjoy the holiday. Finally the front gate is tightly shut and sealed with strips of paper so as to insure that luck remain within the walls.

When all these things have been attended to, the Master or Head of the Household appears in his long robes and kneels before an altar decorated more or less elaborately according to the local custom and the means of the family. This "heavenly table" is hung with a red satin apron, and the principal offerings spread upon it are food, including pyramids of cakes, bowls of rice (in the south), or grain (in the north), red candles, incense, pictures of the gods either in the form of rolled scrolls or a group portrait of the Hundred Deities set up in a wooden standard, and a tablet representing Heaven and Earth.

The New Year services offered in the spirit of thanksgiving for favours in the past and the hope for continued blessings in the year to come, are of very ancient origin. A curious feature is the poster representing the Hundred Gods, a survival of the original "explanatory document" that used to be prepared thousands of years ago by the head of every household. This document, or report on the doings of the family, was first written on bamboo and

Greeting the New Year with music

afterwards on yellow paper, yellow being the national colour of ancient China. It was read aloud and then burned. Later, much later, when people became ashamed of recording their faults which usually exceeded their list of virtues, a blank sheet was used at the sacrifices, and finally, when the Emperor as High Priest assumed the role of mediator for the people's sins and the responsibility of communicating direct with Heaven, the simple folk presented a yellow sheet printed with portraits of the gods and goddesses at their alters.

After prayers have been made before the tablet of Heaven and Earth, the Household Gods next receive offerings and worship with a service practically identical, and then the Ancestors are given their share of reverence.

Wherever space permits, a family will devote a special hall to their Ancestral tablets, plain unpainted strips of wood each marked with the posthumous title of the spirit which it represents and of which it is believed to be the actual dwelling place. The cult of the dead centres in this household shrine and here the New Year feast is spread for the Shadowy Ones in gratitude and reverence. If there be no Ancestral Hall, the tablets are kept in a cupboard or on a shelf and placed upon an altar table only at seasons of worship; but however simply housed, the dead are never forgotten. They are always united to the living in a bond of affection, and whatever the family enjoys is first offered to them; the choicest morsels of the New Year Feast, even the hot towels commonly used to wipe hands and faces after a meal. Believing as they do that the spirits still need food, drink and even money in the Shadow World, and that, if neglected, they feel lonely, it would be cruel not to serve them. After all, the present owes a debt to the past. The forefathers, founders of the homes, have made the families what they are to-day. Therefore, to deny them gratitude and not to supply their simple wants would be ungrateful.

In order that they may share in the New Year festivities, the Tablets remain on their own altar with constantly renewed food offerings for from five days to two weeks and any relative who comes to call greets them before his mortal kin. Meanwhile a specially fragrant incense known as "everlasting" is kept burning near their tablets. Its ash never falls but the stick keeps its shape as it curls round a wire spiral. Some member of the family or a trusted retainer watches night and day to replace each piece as it burns out, so that an uninterrupted stream of fragrance may delight the spirits.

As soon as the first set of religious ceremonies are over the family gather to wish one another a happy New Year. All must greet the Master and Mistress of the Household who seat themselves on stiff chairs while their descendants come and kneel before them, touching their foreheads to the ground. At the same time a dutiful son or daughter murmurs *"ying dang,"* "I ought," an expression equivalent to a promise of obedience throughout the coming year. When grandsons paid their visits to grandparents they used to be given two sticks of sugar cane symbolical of the flag poles formerly put up outside the yamen (office) of an official. This was taken to mean that the boys should obtain a government position —the ambition of every educated Chinese youth.

21

After the family has passed in review, the servants file into the room and greet their employers. Then etiquette relaxes and men and women of the same generation say "happy New Year" to one another without much ceremony, simply bowing with hands joined together and expressing thanks for the New Year gifts each has received.

Much as we do at Christmas, the Chinese make presents at the New Year. Children, servants, and near relations may receive money; women jewellery or rolls of silk. Among the poorer classes practical gifts like a new pair of shoes are considered suitable and flowers, tea, cakes or indeed any kind of food, cooked or uncooked, are offered in all walks of life. A generous man will send his friends a selection of gifts—say a pair of live ducks, several bowls of cooked macaroni and a dozen varieties of cakes, fruits or sweetmeats. He who receives them must, according to the old custom, make a choice, returning a good proportion of what is sent and giving the servant who brings them a tip in proportion to the things accepted. Whoever sends a present must get one of equal value in return and in the whirligig of new year giving it often happens that the eggs from an aunt travel on to a niece, and grandmother's pudding finds its way to the home of a second cousin.

Shortly after midnight, the family sits down to the first of the holiday feasts, known as the "Feast of Re-Union" or the "Making-Up-Feast-to-Say-Goodbye-to-the-Year." All quarrels are supposed to be forgotten or patched up at this New Year supper which symbolises harmony and family unity. Everyone gorges

22

Celebrating the Lantern Festival in a Chinese home

on hot meat dumplings and other dainties and rises from the festal board with a stomach well filled, and at peace with the world.

A short rest, and the "Triple Rites" are performed a second time with the idea of greeting the gods and the Ancestors. The front gate is opened just before dawn and crackers and rockets are set off in quantity until every courtyard and doorstep is littered with spent shells. Thus the New Year's Eve celebrations close in an apotheosis of noise which the Chinese so thoroughly enjoy, and everybody retires for a few hours of much needed sleep.

The first day dawns in silence and peace. Duties are over for the time being. People are tired from the long "Watch Night" and gladly give themselves over to rest and amusement. The streets are quiet and deserted. Few carts or chairs ply for hire because even the humblest coolies take this one day off and custom decrees that it be spent mostly indoors, "each family apart." All shops are closed, likewise theatres and bath houses. The traditional amusements of the day are feasting, gambling, playing musical instruments or simply sitting around in one's best clothes doing nothing, which is in itself an amusement to a hard working people like the Chinese.

The "second day" brings new duties such as the re-opening of the well closed on New Year's Eve, and on the "third" a very important rite must be performed—the worship of the God of Wealth by whom is usually meant *Tsai Chen*, a misty personality who rode a black tiger and hurled pearls that burst like bombs at his enemies.

Peking tradition makes him one of five brothers who stole from rich officials to give to the poor, and the crowds of pilgrims that

24

flock to his temple in the holiday season burn incense before every member of the family at the five fold altars. Indeed so dear to the hearts of the people are the favours of the Money Gods that *Tsai Shen* and his relations are never neglected. Moreover, various additional local gods, fairies and deified alchemists—supposed to aid in distributing wealth—are worshipped in different towns and services are held in honour of some or all of them not only in the temples but in shops and homes.

After the "third day" many people begin their round of "New Year" calls. Shops re-open with a burst of fire crackers, a shaking of the abacus on the doorstep for luck, and an offering of paper money to *Tsai Shen* and company. The life of the streets returns to normal, though a few conservative folk remain indoors till the "fifth day" when the New Year altars are dismantled and the holidays are said to have "broken."

New Year visits are absolutely obligatory to teachers and in-laws as well as to all blood relations. They used to be a terrible tax on families with a large circle of friends. Only high officials were excused from making the round in person and might send their long red paper visiting cards by their servants; but ordinary people were expected to go to all their neighbours, men calling upon men only and their wives feasting with the ladies in the inner apartments. Every caller must be offered food so that by the end of the day hosts and guests were nigh to bursting after their series of feasts in which even the children shared.

Babies in arms accompanied their mothers to the houses of all near relations and older

25

boys and girls joined in the gambling games that often continued till far into the night. Before leaving home the youngsters were carefully warned to speak only "good words" as it was most important that phrases with an unlucky meaning be avoided at New Year time. The mention of death, devils, or malevolent animals would be enough to counteract all the parents' good wishes for luck, riches and peace. Lest a mischievous baby pop out what he must not say, prudent mothers paste a red paper on the wall inscribed with the characters meaning, "Children's words do not count."

New Year taboos included many things besides unlucky words, some being peculiar to a family or even an individual, though the majority were universal. The following are a few examples of the New Year superstitions still found in old fashioned Chinese homes. No meat chopper or other sharp instrument may be used on the "first day." Neither cooking nor sewing are permitted and no strange woman may "pass the gate" until after the fifth.

Simple forms of sorcery are practised in the "inner apartments" usually under the guidance of some old peasant serving woman who remembers the omens and prohibitions she learnt in her childhood when she lived closely associated with Nature in some distant village. Under her supervision the mistress of the house will "sprinkle the vinegar" in all the corners to drive out lurking devils, anoint the doorposts with the blood of a cock for the same reason, or place padlocks as good luck talismans round the necks of the children.

The custom of "observing the year" used also to be common among Chinese ladies. As soon as the new Almanac, prepared annually by the Astrologers appointed by the Emperor, was distributed at the New Year, the family soothsayer would be called to interpret its predictions for the coming twelvemonth.

Poring over this quaint book printed on soft Chinese paper and illustrated with pictures of the gods and mythical animals to explain the letter press, this old man with his long finger nails and tortoise-shell spectacles would read to the women passages that they had not the education to decipher for themselves.

Did they want their fortunes told or their horoscopes cast, he was ready to oblige them. He could also give the correct hours and days for worshipping certain stars and most important of all indicate the lucky and unlucky days for certain enterprises. The "book of the year" guided all the events of their lives. It was dangerous to repair the kitchen stove or even take a bath when the Almanac advised against it.

The underlying reason at the root of many of these customs was undoubtedly to vary the home routine and amuse conservative ladies who remained much within the walls. A woman gad-about soon got a bad name. Exceptional liberty, however, was permitted to matrons and maidens at the holiday season when, accompanied by their female servants, they visited the temple fairs. In the name of religion, amusements were allowed; for after prayers were said to the gods, pilgrims were free to enjoy the secular side, so to speak, of the fair. Beyond the limits of the sanctuary, booths were set up for the sale of toys. Here the children gathered to make their purchases clutching in their tiny hands the cash given them by their elders, choice was slow and difficult with so many tempting things—spears covered with silver paper, soldiers made of crickets, coloured glass tubes that sound a trumpet note, and little figures of old time warriors that dance on a brass tray when the edge is struck with a stick—for the boys; miniature sets of furniture carved in wood, models of Pekingese dogs and mechanical mice that hop when tickled with a hair, for the little girls. Only dolls are lacking, perhaps because in every Chinese family there are so many human dolls that sister always has a younger baby to nurse.

Further along the street of peddler's booths, there would surely be stalls for the sale of jewellery, hair ornaments, and modern novels written in language simple enough for women to understand. Acrobats and story tellers entertained the crowds and open air restaurants furnished an amusing picnic lunch. Because outings were rare, old fashioned Chinese ladies found pleasure even in trifles and these New Year excursions were great events in their dull lives.

The Feast of Lanterns celebrated on the fifteenth of the first moon, used to mark the official end of the holidays. Before this date the lantern shops made a great display. They were crowded with customers buying lanterns to decorate their homes, and toy lamps in the shape of rabbits and frogs or birds with flapping wings to amuse the children. Lantern exhibitions where priceless specimens of lacquer with painted panels by famous artists were on show used to be held in temples and attracted hundreds of visitors. Lantern *fêtes* were given at Court. The most elaborate, according to

28

historic records, took place during the Ming Dynasty at Nanking. Ten thousand lamps floated upon a lake and the effect was so beautiful that legend says the gods came down from Heaven to see it. Ch'ien Lung attempted to rival this festival in the gardens of his summer palace near Peking but no one knows whether he succeeded or not.

Unfortunately the old customs connected with the Lantern Festival are fast dying out. Fewer and fewer "ever burning" lamps are lit by the faithful on temple altars and electric light makes it unnecessary for pedestrians to carry lotus lanterns in the streets at night as they used to do. Only in the country districts are tapers still left burning at the cross roads to guide lost spirits back to their graves. It is rare to see a temple decorated with strings of coloured lanterns. Even the pretty custom of presenting lanterns in the shape of little boys to those who desire sons is falling into disuse, and few hoist the "heavenly lantern" on a mast trimmed with fir branches in the courtyards of their homes.

Now that the Chinese Government is making a determined effort to introduce the Western calendar, it seems inevitable that old Chinese New Year traditions will fall more and more into disuse. As families disintegrate and the sacred traditions of the home are lost, the inner significance of the festival will disappear. The present seems in a fair way to crowd out the past and the new generation ready to sacrifice much that is picturesque and beautiful for much that it practical and ugly. Although a complete return to the order of things is neither likely nor even desirable, one can only hope that the best traditions of the past may be preserved even if they need to be modified.

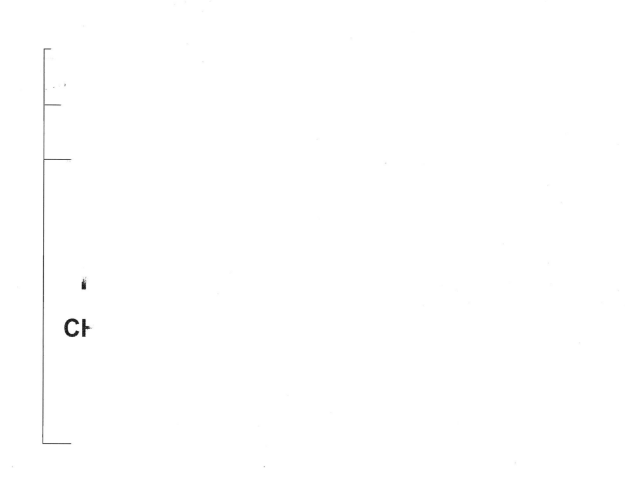

CH